Autumn Moon

Written by Pat Collins
Illustrated by Kerry Gemmill

Rigby

Autumn Moon

With these characters ...

Rodd

Torv

Hera

Hethal

Jojo

"Something strange

Setting the scene ...

It is thousands of years ago, and the winters are growing colder and longer. The eclipse of the moon on a dark arctic night can mean only one thing for Rodd and his family — something bad is about to happen.

When his daughter Hethal falls ill with a mysterious illness, Rodd has only one choice. He must leave his family and travel through the unknown lands to the south, hoping to find something that can save her. But food is short, and the ice and the snow have frozen Rodd to the bone. He needs to find help — fast!

Prologue

Deep beneath the icy snows that still cover much of central Asia and the Siberian plains, lies the hidden remains of an ancient trading route. Known as the "Great Autumn Moon Road," the path was created many years ago when traders from the north and south traveled its course to exchange goods that neither could find or make in their own lands.

Bearskins and fruit, spices and timber, gemstones and silks: all were once carried along the Great Autumn Moon Road.
The trading route changed the lives of those using it forever, as weary travelers traded food and ideas from afar. From primitive hunting and gathering family groups to large, organized trading societies, all had something to offer.
Where it began, no one knows — only that trading started back in the ancient mists of time ...

Chapter 1

Rodd stared upward. Dark autumn clouds
raced across the night sky. An icy chill,
heralding the approaching winter, blew across
the frozen northern landscape. Something
strange was happening to the moon, and Rodd
felt a rising sense of panic. Slowly, the pale
creamy circle was turning a terrifying orange
color. It was the color of dead leaves, decay,

and rust. The night sky was warning Rodd
that something terrible was about to happen.

Rodd hurried his wife and daughter into the
cave that they shared with his brother, Torv.
They huddled together, pressing against the
smoky rock walls for safety. The cave protected
them from the great white bears that had
begun to roam this area, but it could not
protect them from the death of the moon.
A silent terror filled the cave, like thick black
smoke from a smoldering, damp branch.

No one spoke. Even Rodd's daughter, Hethal, who normally chattered noisily, fell silent. No one knew why the moon was the color of an oak tree approaching winter. Would it tumble from the sky, like an autumn leaf? Without the moon, would the night be forever filled with a threatening, blinding darkness?

Rodd and Torv crept back towards the mouth of the cave. They looked up and gasped. The whole moon was still a frightening dark orange color, like the unblinking eye of a dangerous animal. The eerie light made the ice and snow around the cave glow with a chilling flame — but the worse was yet to come.

As the two men watched in horror, the bright round edge to the right of the moon grew darker and darker. Then, before their very eyes, the moon began to disappear. Animals that should have been asleep woke, and the gusty night air was filled with strange, confused cries.

The darkness had now spread from the right edge so that half the moon was in darkness.

Rodd and Torv could do nothing but watch, as the dying glow was gradually swallowed up by the black, arctic night.

"What do you see?" came a whisper from the rear of the cave. Rodd's wife, Hera, was silhouetted by the embers of their fire.

"The moon has died," replied Rodd quietly, so young Hethal would not hear.

Hera crept closer, leaving Hethal to rest by the fire.

"The moon dies every month," she said. "And then a new moon is born."

"This is different," whispered Torv. "The moon goes away slowly, night by night. But this time, it dies as we watch. Look!" Torv moaned in terror.

Rodd, Torv, and Hera stared in silence as the last sliver of the moon darkened. Within seconds it disappeared, and a blackness that no one had seen before descended over the land. A freezing wind blew down from the north with a low, sorrowful moan.

Suddenly, an eerie blue ribbon of light curled and shimmered its way across the northern sky. It danced, shifted, and changed color from blue to deep purple to green.
As soon as it had floated away, another ribbon of light wove its way across the black sky.
Torv and Hera gasped.

"Our grandfather spoke to me about these lights," said Rodd quietly. "In the time when the lands around us were green and fertile, strange lights danced across the sky."

Torv nodded. He, too, remembered a time before the ice came. He remembered warmer days when water flowed in rivers, not glaciers. He remembered their father and grandfather gathering fruits and vegetables from the forests nearby. He remembered when the bears that they tried to avoid had been black and brown, not white.

"Grandfather said the lights were like a waterfall in the sky," Rodd continued. "But he did not say what they meant."

That part of the story was true. Their grandfather had described the lights like that. But what Rodd didn't tell them was even more troublesome. Rodd remembered his grandfather's fearful voice as he had told him more about the mysterious lights.

"The lights mean that there is change in the air. Someone or something will never be the same again," his grandfather had warned.

In a comforting voice, Rodd told Torv and Hera they must all stay warm inside the cave. As they settled themselves beside the fire, Rodd felt deeply troubled and frightened. He remembered the change in their seasons, many years ago, the last time the ribbons of light had sliced through the night sky.

In only a few more seasons, the land had become cold and barren. Great ice sheets from the north had moved slowly toward their lands, and one spring the frozen rivers had not melted. Their lands and rivers lay beneath a permanent blanket of ice.

The fruit and vegetables they gathered from the forest became scarce. The animals they hunted for food grew fewer in number. It was then that the white bears had arrived, prowling the icy land like voracious predators. Life had changed drastically.

Inside the cave, the orange glow of the fire was warming, not like the chilling glow from their autumn moon. Rodd looked at the frightened eyes of Hethal staring up at him. He smiled at his daughter and gently kissed her cheek. Gratefully, she burrowed tightly into the furs that he wrapped around them both. He huddled up against Hera and nodded to Torv. Together, they waited to see what other terrors the long, black night would bring.

Forcing himself to stay awake, Rodd watched and waited while the others fell into an unsettled sleep. What had happened to the moon? What did the streaking lights mean? Would this coming winter be their last? What — or who — was about to change?

Chapter 2

As the glow of the fire within the cave grew dimmer and dimmer, a chilly breeze swirled into the cave. A spark twirled upward, glowing brightly before dying.

Lovingly, Rodd lay little Hethal beside his sleeping wife and, without waking them, he crept over to the embers. Carefully he rearranged the blackened, smoking twigs and laid a curved branch over the top. They must never lose the fire — it was the only thing that enabled them to survive in this harsh climate.

Filled with fear, Rodd crept towards the mouth of the cave. Outside, the black night was still dark, but the lights had finished their dance across the sky. Rodd turned his head to where the moon had once been. He gasped and his heart thumped. He closed his eyes and opened them again to make sure there was no mistake.

Then Rodd grinned as a feeling of relief washed over him.

Hovering high in the sky was a thin creamy curve. Rodd watched in delight as it grew thicker before his eyes. The moon was being born again!

A chorus of birds welcomed the new beginning. The moon was alive again — and so too was the icy landscape.

Rodd crept back inside the cave, Hethal stirring as her father put his finger to his lips.

"Shhh, little one," he whispered. "Everything is well. Do not wake the others."

Hethal smiled and closed her eyes. Rodd lay down beside his family and at last, fell into a deep sleep.

He dreamed of the time before the ice when the forests were always full of birds. Now, they stayed only a short while before migrating southward. Soon, they would be gone again. The winter was a hard time, with few vegetables, no fruit, and little meat. His dreams turned into a hunger nightmare.

"Rodd!"

He leaped up, shaking, staring around wildly. Where was he? What was happening?

"Rodd!" He saw Hera's face. "Just a dream, Hera," he moaned, as his wife tried to relax.

Deep into winter, the temperatures fell even further. The birds disappeared southwards and the night when the moon vanished became a distant memory for Rodd, Torv, Hera, and Hethal. There were now more urgent things to occupy their minds.

Food was desperately short, and the snow around their cave grew deeper. The forest plants that gave them sustenance had died. The winter hunger set in, and the dull ache that spread through their bodies was both painful and hollow.

"This winter is even worse than the last," said Torv, as he returned home empty-handed after a day scouring the forest. "Each year, the snows fall deeper. The white bears grow hungrier and more violent. The skies get darker and the rivers of ice move closer to our home."

Rodd and Hera nodded grimly. A few stringy roots roasted over the fire. The best roots were given to Hethal while the remainder were shared among the adults. But it was never enough.

The lack of fresh food hit hard, and it was becoming even more difficult to find the energy to search for something to eat. The northerly gales continued howling like a great white bear with a spear in its side. Everybody longed for the days when spring would come again.

Then without warning, something happened that no one could explain. First Torv — then Hethal — fell ill with a dreadful sickness that seemed to drain all their energy from them.

Rodd looked at the hollow, sunken faces of his daughter and brother. Their eyes were blackened and their teeth and gums were bleeding from the strange illness. He knew he had to do something. If he didn't, surely they wouldn't survive.

Chapter 3

"We desperately need fresh food, Rodd," said Hera, feeling anxious. "We need fruits and vegetables. Without them, Hethal and Torv will not survive the winter."

Rodd pulled his furs tightly around his shoulders.

"I will follow the birds," he said, trying to sound hopeful. "The birds cleverly find new homes for the winter, where there must be leaves, flowers, and fruit. Otherwise they would all die, too."

Hera nodded and tried to smile. But her heart was heavy with worry and her stomach was tight with hunger.

"Be careful, Rodd," she warned.

Knowing that he must find something with which to fight the mysterious illness, Rodd summoned up the last of his energy and began his journey southward.

For three days, Rodd struggled through the icy, windswept landscape. He kept a watchful eye out for the great white bears. His hair and beard were laced with ice and snow. With each passing day, Rodd grew more and more worried. There was nothing but skeleton-like trees breaking the white blanket that smothered the frozen wasteland. With hands cramped with cold, he dug through the snow, searching for bulbs or soft roots or buried seeds. But there was nothing but soil, frozen as hard as rock. There was no food to be found.

Days passed and still Rodd trudged on southward. He thought of his family, gradually giving into the illness that no-one had seen before. Exhausted, he chewed slowly on small scraps of bark that he peeled from trees and small, lifeless shrubs. The daylight hours grew shorter. He spent the long nights wondering if he would ever see Hethal, Hera, or Torv again.

Rodd grew weaker with each passing day and, as his thoughts became confused, he began to imagine things. In the distance, he saw a small raspberry shrub, bursting with deep purple berries — but when he raced towards the spot, it vanished and was replaced by the wiry, dead branches of a lifeless bush.

Still, he forced himself onwards, for he had to find fresh food. Each step through drifting snow made him dizzy. A foul taste filled his mouth, and when he spat on to the ice, he saw with alarm a shower of tiny red droplets staining the white ground beneath him.

Rodd realized with horror that he, too, was now afflicted with the dreaded illness! Giving up hope, Rodd looked around wildly.

But there, in the distance! Was it? Yes! A tall, green tree shimmered on the horizon. Its branches were weighed down with strange fruits that he had never seen before. He struggled to the life-giving tree, only to see it shrink before his eyes into a lifeless wiry bush. He was confused. Surely this wasn't the same shrub that he had imagined to be bursting with raspberries? Or was it? Had he been walking in circles. He looked behind and saw his footsteps filling with fresh snowflakes. He groaned. He had no idea which way was south anymore.

Suddenly, he heard sounds like metal striking metal. Puzzled, he tried to focus on its source, but the snow muffled the noises. He imagined that he heard voices, and then the voices became those of his father and his grandfather.

Both men were talking of the old days when food was abundant and the ice and snow stayed north beyond the glaciers. Rodd slumped to the ground and closed his eyes.

He imagined mountains and fruit and vegetables and listened without interest to the voices of his ancestors. Wave after wave of weariness swept over him and slowly he fell into an unconscious state. Gradually the whiteness of the ice and snow that surrounded him became replaced by blackness.

Chapter 4

Rodd awoke with a feeling of panic and pain. A stinging sensation filled his mouth and the unbearable burning pain shot up into his jaw. He tried to sit upright, but a pair of hands pushed him down again. He swallowed, and a strange-tasting liquid filled his throat.

Rodd forced his eyes open and slowly focused on his surroundings. A dark figure was standing over him as he felt his mouth fill again with the stinging liquid. Who was doing this? What was this liquid? Was someone trying to poison him?

"Who ... are ... you?" he asked weakly. His voice sounded strangely distant. "What are you doing?"

"Drink," replied the figure. Rodd took a sip from the wooden bowl being lifted to his lips. Trickles of liquid stung his gums again.

"This will make you well," came the voice again. "Drink."

Rodd swallowed. He was now fully awake and he could taste the sweetness of the liquid over the stinging. Greedily he gulped another mouthful. But the blackness took control of his body once more. Rodd sank back into unconsciousness.

When he awoke again, he heard the crackle of a fire. In agony he raised himself on one elbow and stared around. Furs and skins formed a wall around him. The firelight danced eerily on their surfaces. Suddenly from the corner of his eye, he caught a slight movement. He turned his head sharply and saw a dark shape squatting on the floor. Teeth glinted in the firelight. The figure grinned over at him.

"Who are you?" asked Rodd once more. He sat up and instantly every muscle and bone in his body ached.

"Jojo," replied the figure. "Jojo saves your life." And as he grinned his brown, leathery face creased into a hundred deep wrinkles. He was a small, wiry man with thin, hard eyes and thick, black hair.

"Jojo travels from the south," he said. "Lucky for you. Jojo looks for bear. Only find you." Jojo waved at a small bundle of brown bearskins tightly wrapped on the earthen floor of the tent.

Suddenly Rodd remembered why he was there.

"My wife! My daughter! My brother! I need to take some food to them," he cried, pointing to his gums. "This bleeding sickness. They have it, too."

Jojo looked at Rodd. He shrugged his shoulders and shook his head.

"Maybe too late. You *very* sick," he said.

"No, it can't be too late. I must go back! That … that … drink. Was it the drink that saved me?" asked Rodd, struggling to stand up.

The grin vanished from Jojo's face and it was replaced by a frown.

"Jojo save you," he said forcefully, then slowly grinned again. "Drink help. Now you must help Jojo."

Rodd felt his anger rising. He would do anything to return to his loved ones, but who was this man? What did he want? Why didn't he seem to care about Rodd's family?

"How can I help you then?" he asked.

Jojo scratched his head. "Jojo will think. Maybe tomorrow Jojo will tell you."

Rodd sank down again. He felt his energy fading too much to argue. He too had to think.

Rodd forced a smile at Jojo. "Do you have more of the drink?" he asked.

"Plenty," smiled Jojo, pointing towards a large sack made from animal skins. He leaned over, opened the sack, and withdrew something. Rodd's eyes widened, not believing what he saw.

The object that Jojo held was small and perfectly round. It was the color of the autumn moon that Rodd had fearfully watched dying many nights before. The orange object glowed in the firelight.

What was this strange object? Was it a small, magical moon? Did it have special moon-like powers? Rodd stared in amazement as Jojo casually tossed one over to him. With his heart pounding, Rodd caught the orange sphere and pressed its leathery skin beneath his fingertips. He sniffed it, and a bittersweet aroma filled his nostrils.

"Inside, sweet fruit," explained Jojo, looking at Rodd in amusement. "From far south where always sun. No ice, no snow. No bears, either."

"Will you give me some to take back to my family?" pleaded Rodd. "They need this fruit. They will die without it."

"Not Jojo's fault," replied Jojo matter-of-factly. "Maybe you give Jojo something for these fruits? Jojo save you. What you do for Jojo?"

Rodd looked around. What could he possibly give this man? He had nothing. His family had nothing. The land where he lived held nothing of value either. But he needed something, anything, to trade his way out of Jojo's clutches and back to his family. His eyes fell upon the bundle of brown bearskins, and suddenly he had a flash of inspiration.

Rodd nodded towards the bearskins.

"You only have brown skins," he said.

Jojo snorted with laughter. "Bear only brown," he chuckled. "Of course only brown skins."

"How would you like a pure white bearskin?" asked Rodd smiling. Jojo's eyes widened.

"No, no such bear," he said, eyeing Rodd suspiciously.

"As white as the ice and snow," replied Rodd nodding.

Jojo's eyes lit up with excitement. A pure white bearskin. This was unheard of! He knew that in the south this would be valuable.

"Where?" he asked excitedly. "You tell Jojo where!" Rodd shook his head.

"No," he said. "I will take you there." Jojo beamed, and his eyes gleamed in the firelight.

Same as page 20.

Days passed and still Rodd trudged on southward. He thought of his family, gradually giving into the illness that no-one had seen before. Exhausted, he chewed slowly on small scraps of bark that he peeled from trees and small, lifeless shrubs. The daylight hours grew shorter. He spent the long nights wondering if he would ever see Hethal, Hera, or Torv again.

Rodd grew weaker with each passing day and, as his thoughts became confused, he began to imagine things. In the distance, he saw a small raspberry shrub, bursting with deep purple berries — but when he raced towards the spot, it vanished and was replaced by the wiry, dead branches of a lifeless bush.

Still, he forced himself onwards, for he had to find fresh food. Each step through drifting snow made him dizzy. A foul taste filled his mouth, and when he spat on to the ice, he saw with alarm a shower of tiny red droplets staining the white ground beneath him.

In time the bearskin traders who followed Rodd and Jojo would forget how the route became known as the "Great Autumn Moon Road." Now it is also forgotten — but deep beneath the icy snows that still cover much of central Asia and the Siberian plains, lies the hidden remains of an ancient worn path. Perhaps, some day it will be discovered again.

"Orange"

Orange, the color of the leaves that fell —
Orange, the moon that did foretell —
Of an orange sky in an Arctic night —
When orange, the fruit,
Saved us from our plight.